NORTHAMPTON BUSES AND COACHES: THE 1990S AND 2000S

MATT COOPER

AMBERLEY

First published 2024

Amberley Publishing
The Hill, Stroud
Gloucestershire, GL5 4EP

www.amberley-books.com

ISBN 978 1 3981 1586 6 (print)
ISBN 978 1 3981 1587 3 (ebook)

British Library Cataloguing in Publication Data.
A catalogue record for this book is available from the British Library.

Origination by Amberley Publishing.
Printed in the UK.

Introduction

The transport scene in Northampton during the 1990s and 2000s was one of relative calm. Council-owned Northampton Transport (NT) dominated the town network, although United Counties (UC), by then part of the Stagecoach Group, was steadily increasing its presence. Restrictions were not imposed on the 'country buses', which could use all bus stops within the borough boundary. Indeed, some town routes were jointly operated. Post-deregulation the two main operators largely kept to their own areas of the town and both exploited new opportunities as Northampton developed.

The Stagecoach Group purchased United Counties from the National Bus Company in November 1987, the two other divisions of the once large organisation, Luton & District and Milton Keynes Citybus, having already been sold to management buyouts in August that year. Prior to its division the state-owned United Counties operated over a large territory of land-locked England, rubbing shoulders with companies such as London Country, Eastern Counties, City of Oxford and Midland Red. Indeed, Northamptonshire is bordered by nine counties, perhaps inspiring the name United Counties.

The traditional green livery used by UC had all but disappeared by the start of this chapter and following NT's sale to Grampian Regional Transport (GRT) in October 1993 the town's red buses soon received a new livery. A variety of coach operators served the town, many on routes from an assortment of outlying rural villages. Few risked taking the opportunities presented by deregulation to compete against the established operators and thus we will only see a handful of occasions where 'bus wars' were experienced. On two such instances a 'PLC vs PLC' battle took place, each usually following a change of regional division and/or local leadership team. Marketing departments thrived during such periods with jibes such as 'Don't just catch the First Bus, make sure it's the Stagecoach One' appearing at bus stops towards the Eastern District in 2003. Traditional route numbering went out of the window with services '4U' and 'K9' featuring a year later. After each 'battle' calm would quickly be restored and the laminated 'Low fare bus' windscreen boards returned to storage for another day. However, a lasting legacy of some description would follow most of these periods of competition.

More logically, during this period was the introduction of 'Multi-saver' tickets for use on NT and UC services within the borough and a Council-supported all-operator 'Buzz card', which was launched in 2006. For the more adventurous a Sunday Rover ticket had been on offer which covered the whole of East Anglia. At the time of the launch in summer 1996, routes and frequencies were not at the levels on offer in subsequent years. Also, for much of this period NT kept the time-honoured Corporation tradition of not operating on Sundays, with UC running their routes on a tendered basis. Night bus services have only briefly operated around the town on a couple of occasions. In June 1995 UC established 'Z-rota', whose duties involved odd outbound journeys to the Eastern District, the coaches then operating unpublished X48 journeys for BR's Rail Freight staff, taking them to Stonebridge Park. A consortium of organisations supported First's north and south circular routes in late 2002 with three departures on each from Drapery, flat-fares charged and a 'bouncer' allocated to each bus! The services were withdrawn after only a short period with no further opportunities explored.

Whilst conducting research I was amazed how complicated some timetables were during the 1990s. This was journey planning for the savvier passenger in an age of complex paper timetables, face-to-face enquiries (usually to the driver), travel office visits or a phone call to a local depot. Variations on some routes were weekly, daily or even journey specific. For many years NT's local bus timetable resembled a broadsheet newspaper and featured applicable routes run by other operators serving the borough plus a summary rail timetable and an attractive photo on the cover. Today's routings and pattern of service are somewhat more logical and available through national apps on your smartphone, which even show live vehicle tracking. For the enthusiast, this includes scheduling and vehicle-specific information so 'bus spotting' can be carried out from the comfort of your own home!

Vehicle types remained relatively standardised with UC's inherited NBC fleet, which was gradually replaced with Stagecoach Group standard models. NT turned out a uniform fleet until it entered First Bus ownership, when anything would go! The bus industry launched low-floor vehicles during this period and NT was an early user of the type, launching a trio of Volvo B10Ls in late 1995 with European-influenced body-styling. However, it would be the products from UK manufacturers Alexander and Wright that would feature significantly in the town and county. On the subject of trios these were something of a feature with many batches of three delivered to the town's operators. At this time Northampton was always the beneficiary of a continuous supply of new vehicles, step-entrance and low-floor, often resulting in local depot transfers. The inevitable London vehicle cascades would see examples of various vehicle types enter service in the county. UC would even operate a batch of Routemasters acquired from LT in 1988 at a cost of £3k per vehicle! The Bristol VR featured greatly in a number of local fleets, UC being one of the largest users of the type with 218 delivered between 1969 and 1981. NT's batch carried unique body-styling by Alexander and by the beginning of the new millennium many were in use with subsequent owners, some locally, but a significant number overseas. For more details please visit Rob Sly's Bristol Commercial Vehicle website.

As well as looking at Northampton itself we will journey around some of the destinations served from the county town, viewing their associated operations and vehicles. Each of these places has its own distinctive feel and you would be greeted by a different-sounding regional accent when crossing each county boundary. For most, departure would take place from the former Greyfriars bus station. Opened in 1976, this huge concrete structure centralised bus and coach operations in the town and from 1990 became UC's main depot, a purpose for which the building was not intended to the extent used. UC's offices and administration function were at the westerly end of the mezzanine level (roughly between bays 9 and 15) with drivers also using this facility. UC and NT both had small public offices on the main level of Greyfriars with UC's supervisory staff controlling buses and drivers from the same cabin. Potential passengers were required to look carefully for the vehicle's destination blind as the large light box at each bay obscured this important piece of information! The very tired and run-down facility was brought down by controlled explosion on 15 March 2015.

By 2006 all three of the industry's major PLCs were operating in Northampton, Arriva joining with the acquisition of MK Metro, which ran a number of tendered services in the town and county. This meant both of the other companies formed out of the divided UC had owned the new city operator, Stagecoach Group briefly from late 1995 when it acquired Cambus Holdings Group, and Arriva with Luton & District heritage. Milton Keynes Development Corporation had drawn up futuristic plans centred around a monorail but these designs never came to be, and local public transport providers have continued to operate in a challenging environment. Grand public transport plans for Northampton were drawn up in 1996, centred on a rapid transit network, with First Bus initially involved. However, Stagecoach replaced First as development partner at around the turn of the new millennium. None of the plans came to fruition, although some ground preparation was carried out on disused railway lines within the town and nearside guide wheels would appear on several early low-floor buses operated by First. However, these were simply to aid positioning of the bus beside the 'Kassel kerbs'.

Following several local fleet numbering schemes by both major operators national fleet numbers were applied overnight by Stagecoach Group in 2003 and phased in gradually by First Group, region by region, at around the same time. In the main, UC's numbers altered very little, usually just the new 'class code' being added. First's scheme was initially chaotic but by the time Northampton and the Midlands division came to be changed a system similar to that of Stagecoach was in use.

Whilst competition was not a major part of Northampton's transport scene, during this period changes to routes and networks felt almost constant. Cross-town routes were split or merged with others in an attempt to improve reliability. School and contract work came and went as the larger group companies' focus was given to core networks. County Council-sponsored networks featured in later years, which included provision of vehicles. Longer distance inter-urban routes once ran by coaches changed to buses, although connections to neighbouring Stagecoach Group companies' services were well advertised and a Gold Rider (Explorer) ticket covering the whole of south-east England was available. First Group's grand finale in Northampton began in late 2004/ early 2005 when a mass of new vehicles was put to work on an extensive and straightforward town network. Unfortunately, within a year the majority of new vehicles had been transferred to other depots, the routes withdrawn and a gradual run-down of operations ensued. Eventually the operation closed on 14 September 2013. Today Stagecoach Midlands is Northampton's major operator. This new title applied to most of UC's operations, which had been merged with those of Warwickshire. Rugby was the head office of the Warwickshire operation with its roots in Midland Red, perpetuating such quirks as the working week commencing on Saturday and bus 'pull-ins' by work colleagues on a driver's retirement day.

My grateful thanks are due for the photographic assistance of Raymond Bedford, Colin Lloyd, Stewart J. Brown, Nigel Wheeler, David Pike, Patrick Rawlinson, Jeff Jones, Kevin Lane and St Giles Photography. There are some other unattributed shots which I've chosen from my collection. Thank you to Carl Thomas at Pindar Creative for use of the First Northampton map. Thanks also to Bob Jackson for the proofreading and advice, and to Connor Stait and the staff at Amberley Publishing for taking on the project. Most importantly I am indebted to my wife and family for their support, help, understanding and patience throughout this book's creation. For ease, abbreviated terms NT and UC are used throughout the book for references to Northampton Transport and United Counties and their subsequent owners, with several titles being used by both organisations throughout this period.

As fewer people refer to Stagecoach's operation as 'Counties' and with First Northampton (NT) already in the history books we can reminisce this era between NBC ownership and that of today's Stagecoach Midlands. This is the most northerly place where the word 'grass' is not pronounced like 'bass', the rugby players are Saints and football supporters shout 'Cobblers' at their team even when they are doing well. There is a lighthouse, an inland seaside resort and you might find lions in the country. Don't always eat the cheese as some of it is made of wood and thrown at skittles placed on a tabletop. So with Explorer tickets at the ready let's begin our adventure across Northampton and surrounding area.

Welcome aboard 'me duck!'

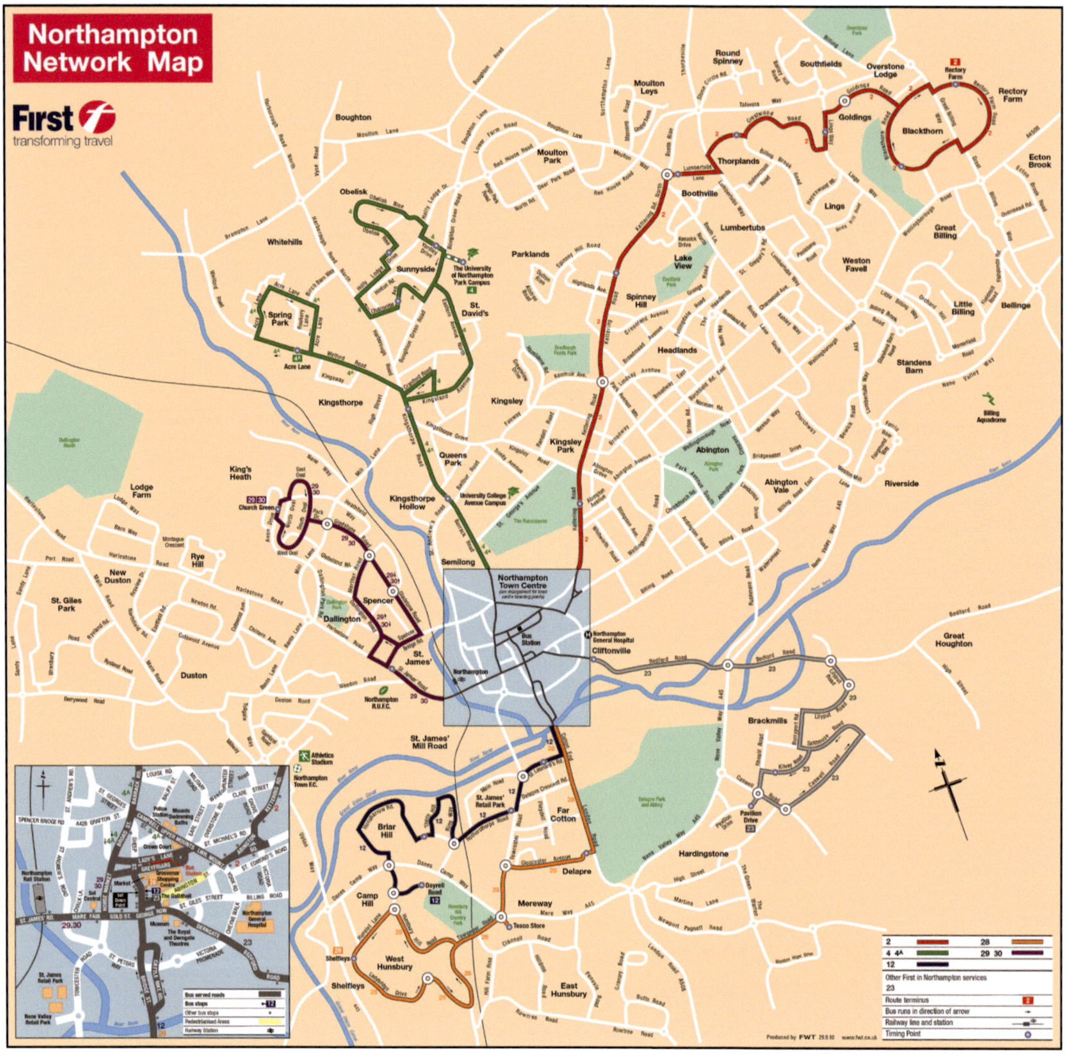

This First Group map dated 2010 shows the layout of the town. By this stage First Northampton only ran a handful of routes which would diminish still before final closure in 2013. With most roads named, it is useful as a street map and details the geography of the town centre.

For many years NT's timetables were published in a large broadsheet newspaper-style leaflet which contained relevant information from other operators within the borough, a summary rail timetable but no map. The edition shown depicts marketing on both buses for Northampton's 800th charter year. GRT kept the tradition going but the final publication was in 1996. The *Passengers' Guide* was produced in 1992 with useful information about NT and the Borough's transport operations.

YORKS
INTER TOWN BUS SERVICES

Effective
25 NOV 1996

Y4

NORTHAMPTON

Great Houghton
Little Houghton
Brafield
Cogenhoe – Hackleton/Piddington
Grendon – WOLLASTON

The reliable, friendly bus service

STOPPING PLACES

YORKS local bus services observe all existing bus stops, where provided, and in addition will stop in rural areas at any point where it is safe and reasonable to do so and no bus stop exists.

In the following places the undermentioned stops only, will be observed:

NORTHAMPTON, Greyfriars Bus Station, Bay 3
The Drapery
Derngate
John Dryden House

GREAT HOUGHTON, White Hart

LITTLE HOUGHTON, Red Lion/Church

BRAFIELD, Billing Road Bus Stop

COGENHOE, Old Peoples Bungalows and Glebe Way
Nene Rise (outward only) & Working Mens Club
Royal Oak and Cogenhoe School

GRENDON, The School

WOLLASTON, South Street Bus Stop

HACKLETON, White Hart, Telephone Box, School

PIDDINGTON, Chapel End/Salcey Rise

Telephone enquiries Northampton 890210

Carrying NCT/NT's highest fleet number under Council ownership, 267 also had the accolade of being the last rear-entrance vehicle built for the home market, being delivered in October 1968. Deliveries of OMO (driver-only) vehicles began in 1973 from fleet number 1, with crew operation remaining at Northampton until May 1985 (using vehicles 261, 266 and 267). Still owned by NT in this July 1993 view at St James depot, the bus would enter preservation at the time of the company's privatisation following a finale working town routes on 30 September 1993. (Nigel Wheeler)

ECW-bodied Bristol VR 794, first registered on 1 February 1973, had been a long-standing Kettering vehicle, as identified by its yellow fleet number plaque. Withdrawal of elderly Bristol VRs soon began under Stagecoach ownership, with those remaining rapidly receiving their new striped livery. An exception was 794, which received a fresh coat of green paint upon request by its regular driver to Perth Head Office, ensuring it remained in service past its nominal retirement date. Finally taken off the books in January 1997, it was sold to the 794 Group, who still own it today. On 14 September that year it was displayed on Market Square during the town's Heritage Weekend.

The first new double-deckers bought by Stagecoach Group for UC arrived on 1 September 1988 in the shape of fifteen Alexander RL-bodied Leyland Olympians seating eighty-seven. Northampton used eight principally on core cross-town route 51 for which they received 'Great Eastern Line 51' branding. Perth registration marks were applied and 627's destination details Sundays-only route 24 to Kingsthorpe, Obelisk Rise. Some of NT's early morning and evening journeys on town routes throughout the week were officially numbered 5xx by UC for administrative purposes. (Stewart J. Brown)

From 1989 NT standardised on the Alexander RV-bodied Volvo Citybus, batches of six being delivered annually. Number 91 is about to enter Greyfriars bus station in November 1990 still devoid of fleet number and local name. Upper-deck headrests would be removed and subsequent batches arrived with this 'luxury' featured only in the lower deck. Working the other principal east–west cross-town route, which for many years ran jointly with UC, the vehicle would clock up nearly twenty years of service, spending its last days in Scotland. (Nigel Wheeler)

Surprise arrivals in October 1992 were fifteen late model Leyland Olympians carrying Northern Counties Palatine bodies. Northampton was allocated the first eleven, which again featured Great Eastern Line branding together with very informative destination blinds. A significant number of 'via' points were on offer to inform intending passengers as demonstrated on 655, the first of the batch, caught setting down at Drapery when only a few months old. All fifteen spent their working lives with UC, with this example later renumbered 14055. In 2010 it was sold to Go Whippet. (Author's collection)

National Express operations were undertaken by UC from their Northampton and Kettering depots. A mixture of coaches was used on the contracts, which from August 1989 featured a unique machine numbered 100. The Yugoslavian-built Famos S315.21 was a budget model of the similar Mercedes-Benz 0.303 imported by dealers Ensign and marketed as 'Ensign Charisma'. The coach wasn't with UC for very long, leaving the fleet by November 1991, but it is well remembered by those who drove it. The camera caught it at King's Cross coach park having worked a journey from Northampton. (Author's collection)

The York family were long associated with the Northamptonshire village of Cogenhoe, from where they established their coach operation in 1924. Several travel agencies were operated in the county along with a handful of bus services, branded as 'Inter-town', many of which were developed around the time of deregulation. In 1988 UC took over most of the routes and by the time of this seasonal view in Victoria Street on 31 December 1996 just the Y4 remained. The regular coach was 62, a Ford R1114 with Plaxton Supreme body carrying battleship name 'H.M.S. Swallow'.

Jeffs of Helmdon were another established family-run coach company, which expanded its operations into neighbouring Buckinghamshire and Oxfordshire by acquiring several smaller local firms. Roe-bodied Leyland Olympian TPD 118X was allocated to the former Basfords Coaches yard at Greens Norton, their closest premises to Northampton. New as London Country LR18, the bus was acquired at the end of 1999 from Oxford Bus Company, who had used it in High Wycombe with identity 978. Having just completed its regular run from Campion School to West Hunsbury on 22 April 2002 it is seen at Hilldrop Road, East Hunsbury. Today the vehicle operates in a non-PCV role as a promotional roadshow vehicle.

NT were at the cutting edge of low-floor operations, launching a trio of Alexander Ultra-bodied Volvo B10Ls on 11 October 1995. Routes 27 and 28 were the lucky recipients of the vehicles, which originally wore a local version of parent Grampian's 'Advance S.E.' livery. By the time of this scene on 15 August 2000 all three had received standard First Group low-floor livery along with internal refurbishment. Awaiting custom at the newly established bus stop at St Benedict's Mount on Hunsbury Hill Road 41 (N41 RRP) was making its way around route 27's loop of West Hunsbury and Shelfleys. In 2003 it received 'national identity' 61242 after transferring to Manchester. Two years later all three, along with others of the type, would return to Northampton!

The next operator in Northampton to launch low-floor vehicles was Country Lion in August 1997. Another trio of vehicles, this time featuring the Dennis Dart SLF chassis, each carried different bodywork. Previously a demonstrator with Plaxton, N305 DHE was acquired when only a year old carrying that manufacturer's Pointer bodywork. Caught departing Greyfriars on 3 September 1997 on contracted route 6 towards Lumbertubs estate, its low-floor stablemates were both delivered new, registered P4 and P5 CLN and featured Marshall Capital and East Lancs Spryte bodies respectively.

UC were not too far behind, joining the low-floor revolution on 1 November 1998. Nine Alexander ALX200-bodied Dennis Dart SLFs were delivered to Group specification carrying national brand name 'Lo-Liner' (a registered trademark). In partnership with Northampton Borough and County Councils' infrastructure improvements featured along routes 15A and 15B to which the vehicles were allocated. Route 15, which had previously terminated at Bush Hill, was extended east to Weston Favell Centre and Blackthorn terminating on Beaumont Drive, a road not previously served by buses. 456 is seen on Drapery on 4 May 1999.

NT launched six vehicles powered by compressed natural gas (CNG) on 26 June 1997, for which two pumps were installed on the forecourt of St James depot. Again featuring Volvo B10L chassis with Alexander Ultra body, their initial routes were the cross-town 29 and 79 from Kingsthorpe, Acre Lane to Ecton Brook, although the latter terminus was soon changed to Kings Heath. P503 MVV is on Marefair on 30 September 2000 passing Sol Central, then under construction. Originally numbered 503, it had recently changed identity to 46 and would later become 60003. The batch was plagued with reliability issues and all were withdrawn before their tenth anniversary.

UC's new vehicle order for 1999 consisted solely of a trio of Alexander ALX200-bodied Dennis Dart SLFs, to the same layout and design as the previous batch but with bus seats. Delivered on 16 August 1999, they were originally to be registered T462–4 ONV. However, as their arrival was after the introduction of the new annual registration mark they were changed to V462–4 TVV as evidenced by 462 on Rothersthorpe Road on 3 September 1999.

Following the creation of First Bus in 1996 a 'standard' vehicle was sought soon after for use across its constituent fleets. The low-floor products offered by Wright of Ballymena would prove popular with the Group, such as the Axcess-Floline, which was paired to Volvo and Scania chassis. NT received three of the latter in April 1998 from a batch of six shared with Leicester, taking their fleet number series and registered in that city. This attractive design was a vast improvement on the products received beforehand and this rear view of 343 at Greyfriars in May 1998 displays the Group-wide advertising campaign worded in a similar style to that used by Toyota. The R-registered trio moved on to Eastern Counties in May 1999 and subsequently to Glasgow.

Weston Favell Centre (WFC) opened on 29 October 1974, the shopping and district centre becoming the hub of routes serving the developing Eastern District. The main building sat over a large car park with bus stops located on Billing Brook Road accessed by escalators and ramps. The stops on each side of the road were not always served in a logical pattern; the 'Emmanuel Church' side was mainly served by town-bound services, and demonstrating this on 3 October 1997 we see UC Volvo Olympian 689 heading in that direction. However, NT's services 3 and 7 to Rectory Farm served the stop after running from the town centre.

The chassis type of UC's Northampton midibus allocation received between 1993 and 1996 alternated numerous times between the Dennis Dart and Volvo B6. All carried Alexander's Dash bodywork. Volvo B6s 422–431 were delivered to Northampton in October 1993 with only 422 entering service, the others being utilised elsewhere within the Group. Another batch carrying the numbers 423–430 was delivered to Huntingdon from July 1994, the first three transferring to Northampton in August 1996. Compare the angular lines of 423 with that of the Bristol LH training bus behind in this 16 September 1998 view.

Small batches of unusual single-deckers were seemingly a feature in Northampton, none more so than a unique vehicle delivered to NT in March 1992. Originally planned to be a coach, 115 materialised as an East Lancs 2000-bodied Volvo B10M to NT's higher interior specification with forty-seven dual-purpose seats. Looking smart when viewed at St James depot in July 1993, the vehicle would shake and rattle its way through a career at Northampton, eventually to be renumbered 66615 with First and reseated with fifty-one bus seats. It was scrapped in 2008, with the diagonal radiator badge, signifying its Volvo pedigree, remaining in situ for its final journey to Barnsley. (Nigel Wheeler)

Delivery of fifteen Northern Counties Palatine-bodied Volvo Olympians followed a matter of months after their Leyland counterparts. All were a firm feature of core cross-town routes 1 and 51, with penultimate example 684 turning from Gold Street to Drapery on 6 August 1997. The side advert displayed details of the recently privatised rail service offered by French-owned Connex, which ran from Rugby through Northampton to Gatwick. Latterly based at Kettering, the end of step-entrance operation saw the vehicle sold to St Nicholas Primary School in the Oxfordshire village of Old Marston for use as a library.

Arriving at Northampton in November 1997 were nine Alexander RL-bodied Volvo Olympians which featured updated bodywork details including larger destination screen and split-level entrance steps. The wheel trims were in fashion at the time and featured on all types. Their primary duties, as with most new deliveries, were on routes 1 and 51 and 697 heads up Drapery on 8 March 1999, passing bus stops and kerbs which were also being updated.

Under First Bus control thirteen school contracts were awarded by the County Council in March 1996 with a similar number of vehicles being drafted into Northampton from fellow Group companies to operate them. All received the GRT-influenced livery, fleet names and local destination blinds before use, giving a uniform look as evidenced on former Leicester East Lancs-bodied Dennis Dominator working along Randall Road, Kingsley, soon after acquisition. Previously numbered 183, a new 'class' was applied at Northampton, making it 202. From April 1996 route 13 was added to the low-floor diagrams performed by the Volvo B10Ls, which interworked with routes 27 and 28. Conventional buses would also work specific journeys on these services as detailed in timetables and publicity material. (David Pike)

Acquired from Eastern National in September 1998 were four Duple Dominant-bodied Leyland Tigers new to West Yorkshire PTE. All received the single-deck version of the cream-based livery with maroon and red relief as shown on EWR 653Y, numbered 410, another new series shared with Leicester which denoted single-deck step-entrance vehicles. Route 28 was a cross-town service when this 4 May 1999 view was captured at Drapery. Withdrawn just over a year later, the vehicle would go on to work for Sheffield Mainline as their number 82.

Route 8 ran a meandering path from the town centre through Abington Vale and Kingsley to St David's estate at Kingsthorpe. From 9 August 1998 the majority of the journeys on the hourly service were contracted to UC with NT retaining a couple at peak hours extended to All Saints School and Moulton Park. New to Midland Scottish as MRM37, Alexander RL-bodied MCW Metrobus ULS 637X was numbered 265 and acquired from Leicester. On 23 May 2000 it should be standing time at Cranford Road and not Yelvertoft Road, as shown, which was only served by UC journeys.

Joining the local scene at the end of 2002 was Midland Routemaster who operated in Northampton and MK. Their seven journeys on route 8 took the same path as their predecessors but terminated instead at Links View, not serving Kingsthorpe or St David's. The 8A, as depicted, ran via The Mounts, Regent Square and St Georges Avenue to reach Links View and on 25 April 2003 former Unibus Leyland National XAL 485S, new to Trent, awaits its next departure from Bay H. No two buses wore the same livery, with only one carrying a fleet name. However, from day one the company's excellent website could be accessed.

Confidence of Leicester loaned Midland Routemaster two vehicles, Leyland Atlantean KSA 183P (which was subsequently bought) and East Lancs-bodied Leyland Olympian RBO 510Y, which was new to Cardiff Bus in their bright orange livery. The bus had previously been used in Northampton in April 1999 when loaned to NT following a vandal attack at St James depot. On 14 May 2003 it was working its way around Abington Park on Park Avenue South heading towards Links View.

NT had a batch of six similar East Lancs-bodied Leyland Olympians which were new in 1984. They were to dual-door layout, the last double-deckers bought new by the organisation to this configuration. The first of the batch arrives at Greyfriars working principal north–south route 26 in November 1990. Despite being newer then their Bristol VR stablemates, all six were transferred to Edinburgh in 1994 when owned by GRT. (Nigel Wheeler)

Thirty Alexander RV-bodied Volvo D10M 'Citybuses' were received between 1989 and 1993, with locally associated names featured on each of these very reliable vehicles. First of the July 1989 trio, F86 DVV, new as 86, was named 'Queen Eleanor'. By this 4 August 2000 view bus seats had replaced the original high-backed seating upstairs, although extra light for the upper deck was still provided by the three skylights. It would soon to depart Camp Hill on an AM-peak short-working to Greyfriars only.

Parklands and Links View estates could almost be considered peninsulas with both accessed by a linear road and buses using a turning circle at the end. Incidentally the two terminal points could be viewed from each other. NT had begun to withdraw services from both in the early 2000s, after which Midland Routemaster proudly served each estates individually until their operation suddenly ceased on 28 July 2003. From 3 November 2003 MK Metro won the tender for route 11, running hourly serving both estates using brand new Optare Solo 24 (YN53 SVG), which simply carried 'Metro' names and route branding. The bus ran dead to and from its Wolverton home and was viewed on 27 August 2005 at Parklands turning circle. Later painted in the purple route 8 scheme at MK, it became Arriva The Shires 2443 serving until 2018.

Having run their own bus service during 2003 and 2004, using sixteen-seat Ford Transit minibuses, a more frequent and conventional service returned to University College Northampton (UCN) in September 2005. MK Metro won the tender and route 21 initially served both campus sites linking them with the town centre. New to Limebourne and named Dartmouth Castle, Caetano Compass-bodied Dennis Dart SLF 62 (T408 LGP) works diagram N2 on 14 October 2005 at the newly opened bus stops at Park Campus. As can be seen, the main competitor to the service was the car, with parking areas and local side streets filled on a daily basis. Souls Coaches took over the routes in 2010 and the whole Park Campus site has since been redeveloped for housing.

Routes 40/A ran between the villages of Nether Heyford and Moulton via Northampton, the cross-town service being a scheduling convenience rather than a popular link. 657 (later 14057) heads along Lady's Lane towards Moulton on 7 July 1997, its ultimate destination blind having slipped to show a more unusual and seldom-used location. Good use was often made of the 'via' blind making for a most informative display.

NT's route 12, one of four competing services introduced on 16 August 1993, linked the town centre to Moulton Leys and Moulton village every thirty minutes between 8 a.m. and 6 p.m. New in October 1986 were a pair of high-spec East Lancs-bodied Volvo D10Ms. Originally numbered 1 and 2, the duo were utilised more greatly on bus work during their lives renumbered 101 and 102, with the latter about to enter Greyfriars on 20 August 1993. The additional vehicle requirement that summer was achieved by putting six new vehicles on the road ahead of their planned introduction date and utilising the coach and low mileage fleet. The competing routes of both operators had ceased by 10 December 1993.

Under First Group ownership NT would return to Moulton Leys from April 2002 on Sunday-only route 3A. Wright Eclipse-bodied Volvo B7L 355 would run around Manning Road heading for town on 9 February 2003. Drivers on Sundays worked six-hour turns, the 3A interworking with routes 5A and 30. New as 714 in Manchester for Commonwealth Games duties, it was the first of the type to arrive at Northampton on 14 August 2002. Manchester's 7xx numbers were changed on 7 October 2002 to the local 3xx series.

November 1994 saw competition return to the streets of Northampton with Trinity Bus & Coach of Brackley bravely starting routes against both of the town's 'PLCs'. Five former Midland Fox Rootes-bodied Ford Transits entered service in this smart livery with C527 TJF still carrying its former owner's fleet number plaque M127 on the radiator grille. The lucrative Eastern District was served by two routes and at WFC on 16 March 1995 the minibus makes a quick getaway ahead of the competition. NT's Volvo 114 works their retaliatory route 29 running every twenty minutes and following a similar path to that used during the 1993 'bus war'. Trinity was confined to bays 1 and 2 at Greyfriars and only managed to survive until 15 August 1995. However, their legacy saw NT and UC keep some of the routing used on competing services to enhance their established networks. (Jeff Jones)

New to Ribble, a pair of Leyland National 2s were acquired from Cumberland in March 1993 for a Park & Ride (P&R) contract in Bedford. Classified as 'midibuses', by early 1996 LFR 864X, numbered 501, had become part of Northampton's allocation, adding some much needed variety to the depot. It worked all manner of duties including Coachlinks services and in early 1998 was caught at Wellingborough Road by Booth Lane South whilst thundering towards Blackthorn. As seen earlier, route 15 had been recast to become a cross-town service, which was also extended to the Eastern District replacing route 50, which had been established to compete with Trinity Bus & Coach.

The Lo-Liner brand name was discontinued with the introduction of the Stagecoach Group 'beach ball' livery. The WFC bus stops had been extended, refurbished and numbered with clearer signage and timetable cases also added. Despite that, the routing of the services still seemed confusing to prospective passengers at this important and busy location. 457 (S457 CVV) is heading to its easterly terminus of Beaumont Drive on 16 March 2002.

Country Lion, established in Northampton in 1962, runs a varied fleet of coaches and buses on local contracts, private hire and a tour programme. Vehicles are smartly turned out as can be seen on Plaxton Excalibur 350-bodied Volvo B10M A18 CLN, registered new to the company, caught resting at WFC between free bus duties on behalf of Tesco on 17 September 1998.

Route 20 served the full length of Billing Road to reach WFC and ultimately Southfields every thirty minutes. In summer 1992 Volvo Citybus 91 'Knights Templars' heads past some stately town houses which face Northampton General Hospital. (David Pike)

Sister vehicle 93 unloads at St Giles Street post office on 20 March 1998 with a journey from Southfields. The route no longer crossed the town to Kingsthorpe and Acre Lane with that section covered by Gasbus routes 29 and 79. The driver is changing the destination to Kings Heath, routes 2 and 10 being interworked with vehicles on route 20. Its GRT livery looks smart with 'Nene Navigation' name still applied along with a 'First' vinyl, but no local identifiers.

Spring is very much in evidence at the point where Bewick Road seamlessly becomes Billing Road East. From 15 April 1996 three buses per hour linked Ecton Brook with the town centre on routes 29 (later 69) and 79, their journey times reduced by not serving WFC. The Gasbuses had briefly performed Billing Road services from 1997, their use long discontinued by 21 April 2001 when 129 (K129 GNH) heads towards Abington Vale and town centre.

Exemplifying new route 5 at the Dulverton Road stop on 20 June 2001 was former Capital Citybus Alexander Dash-bodied Volvo B6 438 (L680 RMD), still awaiting application of its magenta fade-out vinyl, one of a number used by Northampton and Leicester at this time. The bus would make the next right turn to enter Riverside Retail Park via a transponder-operated bus gate.

From January 2002 UC and NT competed on the significant cross-town route 1, which had previously been shared and co-ordinated. UC established a separate rota of drivers for the route, although no vehicles were branded and any type could operate the service. This included elderly ECW-bodied Leyland Olympians, with eight of the ARP-X batch allocated to Northampton at the time of this 14 December 2001 scene. Complete with 'beach ball' logo, 604 (later 14004) departs the fare-stage stop at Allan Road, which had been resited from a point just ahead of the red car.

In September 2003 eleven Northern Counties Palatine-bodied Volvo Olympians, new to Stagecoach Selkent, transferred from Cambridge. The large arrow points to the tidy single-door conversion of 16431 (VLT 255, N331 NGK), which was 831 at Cambridge and V331 in London. Seven received former Routemaster registrations and all featured excellent London-style local destination blinds. To coincide with National Car Free Day, Monday 22 September 2003, UC ran a week of promotions with the details of one such offer applied to the Cambridge P&R cream-base livery.

Northamptonians using NT's services by the late 1990s had become accustomed to their bus turning up in any colour scheme imaginable, a far cry from the Corporation red bus era. Following the once-in-a-lifetime floods of April 1998 numerous vehicles were hired from fellow First Group companies, some remaining longer-term as mechanical attention was given to the native fleet. From Sheffield Mainline was Duple Dominant IV-bodied Leyland Tiger 63 (YPD 103Y), new to London Country, which also served with Sheafline. Captured at Abington Square on 21 April 1998 whilst working route 14 to Parklands, the bus would return north by mid-May. (Patrick Rawlinson)

Main-line vehicles were again on loan to NT between July and October 2002, this time Wright Renown-bodied Volvo B10BLEs. A number of transfers took place prior to the arrival of the twenty-five Volvo B7Ls from Manchester, which would finally stabilise the fleet. With a full set of NT blinds, 785 (R785 WKW), from the pre-First Group batch, was seen on Wellingborough Road on 25 July 2002 whilst running dead to Rectory Farm. NT withdrew from this significant road in April 2002, returning with a vengeance every ten minutes in late 2004 on route 52 using new vehicles. By 23 July 2005 that service and the buses were withdrawn.

From 27 July 2003 drastic service revisions took place to UC's Northampton town network. Route 1 remained cross-town but severely cut at the Duston end and re-routed in the Eastern District with one-time 'Great Eastern Line 51' being withdrawn altogether. By April 2004 the old pattern was reinstated as the 1 and 1A operating up to every ten minutes. Route branding was introduced in January 2006 when the east and west routes were split. Eleven Transbus Dart SLFs were delivered in 2004, seven of which received Group-standard branding for the easterly route 'one' running up to every eight minutes. 34585 (KX04 RUW) has completed another day's work and awaits a run through the wash in this atmospheric view at Greyfriars. (Author's collection)

With stability restored, route 'one' would go on to become the depot's most profitable and by 2009 twelve ADL Enviro 300-bodied MAN 18.220s were received to upgrade the fleet. Their branding was to a new style, which also featured fare information for Northampton's all-operator 'Buzz card'. 22841 was seen away from home on 5 July 2009 at the one-time Viscount depot on Lincoln Road in Peterborough on an enthusiasts tour.

In 2006 the Duston routes became 9 and 9A, the suffix letter denoting the direction of travel around the old and new estates of Duston. Running up to every ten minutes, the vehicle type initially used was somewhat older than its easterly counterpart, with eight Alexander ALX200-bodied Dennis Dart SLFs transferred from Peterborough. They were from a batch new to Oxford, with this example once numbered 813. Stagecoach East adopted a combined fleet numbering system from April 2002 where the bus briefly carried number 213 prior to becoming 33813 in the national scheme. In late 2007 it was working the anti-clockwise route 9 and about to enter Greyfriars. (Nigel Wheeler)

Receiving an upgrade in May 2008 the 9 and 9A saw another chassis type introduced to the depot, paired to the familiar-looking lines of the ADL Enviro 200. Seven MAN 14.220 were received, which formed part of a larger batch also being delivered to former Midland Red South depots at this time. Six were branded, including 39695 (KX08 HRC) at Black Lion Hill beside the railway station on 24 June 2008. The surrounding roadworks would include relocation of the bus stops to a position behind the bus. In conjunction with the railway station rebuild the layout was remodelled again in 2013, becoming confusing and cluttered. Trams once ran along this section of highway from Weedon Road or St James depot to and from the town centre.

UC operated sixty-two Alexander AM-bodied Mercedes-Benz 709Ds, with ten allocated to Northampton. All carried 'Street Shuttle' branding, the name originating at the time of privatisation and also used by MK Citybus. Contracted Beacon Bingo services played a significant role, with a number of local towns and villages served to bring custom to their Weedon Road site. A bingo membership card was required for free travel on the 650, which operated off-peak Monday to Saturday between Drapery and the bingo hall, some 2 miles away. Whereas bingo organisations' marketing departments nowadays seek a younger audience, a more 'traditional' crowd boards 377 at Drapery on 4 May 1999.

Having had a chauffeur-driven Mercedes on the outbound journey, return travel on Saturday 24 July 1999 was the last of the Northern Counties Palatine-bodied Volvo Olympians, 685. This was the only example of the batch to carry an L-JBD registration, although the 1996 deliveries would carry the same suffix letters.

Just past St James Square we arrive at St James depot, home to NT's operations from 1903 to 2013. This large site was extended over the years and housed offices, workshops and undercover parking for the whole fleet. By 1997 just over 100 vehicles were allocated here and the rear of the depot was also utilised for parking. In July 1993 Volvo Citybus 90 looks magnificent in the final version of the company's red and cream livery, standing in front of the office and administration block which would later be rented out as private offices. (Nigel Wheeler)

NT received a smart Duple 300-bodied Volvo B10M in July 1988 principally for use on route 60 to Guilsborough. Three more of these high-spec vehicles arrived in November 1989, being utilised initially on a mix of private hire and contracts with occasional use on service bus work. Their use increased significantly from 1993 in the run-up to the company's privatisation and 112 works one of the Mereway 'circular' routes during summer 1992, passing All Saints Church at Wood Hill. Becoming 66612 with First Group it moved to Worcester in August 2003 and later operated with Premiere Travel of Nottingham and Baker Bus, Roydon.

Making a similar manoeuvre during the early days of Firstbus ownership on 7 July 1997 was Volvo Citybus 126, the last of the 1992 batch, wearing full GRT livery. Circulars 18 and 19 terminated at Mereway Tesco and were later replaced by simpler and more user-friendly route patterns. In August 2006 the bus transferred to Worcester, later becoming Diamond Bus 42565 when that company took over some of First's operations. It was eventually scrapped in September 2013.

The London and Towcester roads were served by UC's longer southern circulars 30 and 31. By 6 August 1997 they had become 15A and 15B when the vehicle depicted was working the clockwise 'B' turning onto Sheep Street from Greyfriars. Arriving in December 1996 to enhance the revised town network were Dennis Darts 450-2, which featured the restyled Alexander Dash front end. P452 KRP would later become 32008, seeing service at Bedford and Nuneaton depots.

January 2006 saw the launch of the Northampton Borough 'Buzz' brand, which featured standardised bus stop and timetable material together with a range of tickets issued and accepted by all operators in the borough. A number of 'Pay Point' retail outlets also sold the tickets, particularly those of higher value. Abington Street, one of Northampton's major thoroughfares, had been pedestrianised in 1985 and 27 October 2006 saw 34773 (KX55 UDE) the last of a trio of ADL Darts with ADL Pointer 2-bodywork was promoting Buzz Card's Pay Point options. The statue alongside the bus commemorates Professor Francis Crick and James Watson's roles in discovering the helical structure of the DNA molecule. (Raymond Bedford)

NT received a trio of Wright Access Floline-bodied Scania L94s in December 1999, becoming the last to carry local Northampton registration marks under the old DVLA system. They replaced three older examples which had transferred to Leicester following a fire at Abbey Park Road depot. Routes 69 and 79 were created in April 1998, being the eastern-end split from the Acre Lane Gasbus services. No longer advertised as low-floor, it was a luxury for passengers on 14 December 1999 to have brand-new 364 working in wintry conditions at the Wellingborough Road end of Ecton Brook Road.

First Group received seventy-five Wright Eclipse-bodied Volvo B7Ls registered between May and July 2002 in Manchester, for use on Commonwealth Games contracts. Upon completion they were dispersed to other depots, with Northampton receiving twenty-five. The smart lines of the bodywork were hampered by the chassis design of the B7L, which created an awkward internal layout. They served the town well for nearly a decade before being replaced by older stock on the run down to the depot's closure. MV02 VCX still carried its Manchester fleet number on 19 September 2002 when laying over on Great Billing Way prior to beginning a day's work on route 2. Later numbered 335, then 66344, it would transfer to Norwich in 2012.

In early 1993 five Plaxton Premiere 350-bodied Volvo B10Ms were transferred from East Midlands and Rainworth Travel to Kettering depot. From the summer 1993 timetable this was now the sole base of UC's National Express work with a handful of routes being operated. Loading at Greyfriars 'express bay' 27 on 16 September 1998 was 92, working the cross-country 348 between Corby and Bristol. None of the batch, all new to Parks of Hamilton, ever carried the company's cherished registration marks.

Blending in well, with local Coachlinks names and registration mark A729 ANH, was 126 laying over at Greyfriars on 17 March 1998. Carrying a Plaxton Paramount 3200 body and fitted with a manual gearbox, the origins of the coach were somewhat different to the native Leyland Tigers of similar appearance. This Volvo B10M was new in 1983 as A800 TGG to Stagecoach Perth for the company's pioneering cross-border express services. One of three acquired in May 1988, subsequent identities 4009 SC, A332 ANH and WLT 908 were carried. National Express work was eventually followed by local inter-urban routes, then school contracts and finally training duties for the latter part of their lives at UC. All were withdrawn by June 1998.

The Coachlinks fleet replacement began in February 1993 with five Plaxton Premiere Interurban-bodied Volvo B10Ms delivered to Huntingdon and Bedford depots. 152 (K152 DNV) was captured in 1997 taking Bedford depot's Bowls Club to a fixture, such sports and social clubs still very popular at this time. Later numbered 52122, this coach and its sisters would enjoy long careers, with some having a 'second life' as seventy-seater school buses for contracts in Bedford. (Author's collection)

'If you are paying for an advert make it stand out' was perhaps the logic behind Airflow's day-glo schemes featured at Northampton in the mid-1990s! Compare this livery to the more genteel UC green applied to Bristol VR 794 at Showbus, Duxford, in 1995. The Northern Counties Palatine-bodied Volvo Olympian 677 would receive its nightly wash at Greyfriars and not the Duston-based garage advertised. (Author's collection)

Fellow Volvo Olympian 681 received a scheme in April 1996 promoting Northampton Markets, part of a wider campaign at the time extolling the virtues of traditional UK markets. The livery remained for a couple of years with Victor the Market Lion's speech bubble changing seasonally – a Christmas message is still displayed in this 31 December 1996 view. The gloom of Greyfriars bus station can be appreciated as can how close together UC vehicles were parked at the facility, which was never intended to be a garage.

Standard fleet colours featured on the front end of some otherwise overall schemes as exemplified by 16694 (R694 DNH), new as 694 in October 1997. This scheme for Marie Curie Cancer Care was applied in January 2008 and was frequently loaned to the charity's local branch for use at fundraising events. On 8 March 2008 it was on Abington Street.

NT's OPO double-decker was the Alexander AL-bodied Bristol VR, with thirty-six delivered between 1977 and 1978. Prolonged lead-times during construction caused the batch to be registered out of sequence. Fearsome automatic gearboxes featured together with NT's trademark dual-door layout, three large upper-deck skylights and curved rear roofline. Six would be withdrawn per year from 1989, replaced by the Volvo Citybuses. Following privatisation in 1993, no further examples were withdrawn, with ten remaining in use until 1999. In July 1993 the lowest-numbered example was 48, pictured at St James depot. (Nigel Wheeler)

In 1991 NT sold three Bristol VRs to local coach operator Jeffs of Helmdon and on 3 April 2000 two were still in use on school contracts from Greens Norton depot. The names of the companies Jeffs had acquired over the years were retained and applied to a unified livery, which featured a 'leaping deer'. 66 was unique in having an East Lancs upper deck rear fitted following fire damage. The depot site is now a housing estate.

Another trio which stayed local to Northampton went to Brittain's Coaches based at their Southbridge depot, premises previously occupied by Yorks Coaches and, later, Cunningham's. On 16 March 1995 PBD 42R was working a school duty at WFC a matter of months before Country Lion bought the operation. Previously NT's 42, a full set of their destination blinds remained in use. (Jeff Jones)

All three were repainted by Country Lion and their duties would see them occasionally perform the company's service bus work. On 17 March 1998 VVV 61S, also retaining its NT blinds, works lunchtime shuttle bus 108 to Barclaycard offices. Bay 3 at Greyfriars was used by this half-hourly route, with other services to Brackmills available from St Giles Street Post Office. All three were withdrawn in 2002.

In order to upgrade UC's double-deck fleet Stagecoach Group acquired twenty-seven ECW-bodied Bristol VRs from Devon General. One of the first pair to arrive in November 1988 was FDV 812V numbered 734 (originally 1180 with DG). With large numbers of new Leyland and Volvo Olympians allocated to Northampton depot the type did well to survive until 1999, although their use on core town services decreased from the early 1990s. On 3 September 1999 Fleetlink of Liverpool would collect the withdrawn vehicle from Rothersthorpe Avenue. By June 2003 it had emigrated to Rome, operated by Sistemi Bibliotechario Castilli Romani as a mobile library.

UC's remaining Bristol VRs ended their days at Bedford, with eleven still in use at the time of this 22 September 1999 scene at the town's bus station. Northampton's Mercedes Benz 709D 377 carries 'Street Shuttle' branding while working an MK outstation duty, whilst Bedford's Volvo Olympian 567 displays 'Coachlinks' on its front panel. Bristol VR 962 had been a long-standing member of Northampton depot, delivered in April 1981 and clocking up twenty years of service with UC. Since April 2008 it has been in use with Party Buses, Denver, Colorado, USA.

Another Bristol VR to serve Northampton for the majority of its life was 911 (FRP 911T), new in April 1979. Receiving its corporate stripes in January 1990, the vehicle spent its final months based at Corby. In similar vein to Greyfriars, Corby's bus station surely ranked highly as a most depressing concrete structure, although escalators linking it to the above Queen Street looked quite novel. 911 lays over in the outside parking area on 7 August 1997 while working long-established contract route 699 for RS Components.

Jeff's Coaches favoured Caetano Algarve bodywork as exemplified on K97 UFP, one of a pair new in March 1993 with Dennis Javelin chassis. The fifty-five seater was a good crowd shifter and on 20 October 2001 was one of a number of coaches hired by 'Cobblers' supporters to attend a match against Queens Park Rangers. Awaiting the final whistle at nearby Ariel Way coach park, the vehicle is in company with Northamptonshire-based Jesus Army's East Lancs-bodied Scania K92 E108 JYV, new to Grey Green and one of several buses and coaches owned by that organisation. This area has now been redeveloped as Westfield shopping centre and venue 'Exhibition London'.

Yorks Coaches were fond users of the Kassbohrer Setra S215HD, most of which were bought new. 98 (TVY 659, C98 RVV), returning home from a day trip to Chester, carried the name 'HMS Beaver' and was one of sixteen examples in use when this 16 August 1993 view was taken at Hilton Park services. The livery complements the smart lines of the German-built integral coach.

When owned by the Bowen Group, new stock for Yorks arrived in the shape of the Spanish-built Noge Catalan coupled to MAN chassis. Some tri-axle examples were employed, as shown in this view of S604 VAY enjoying a day at the ever-popular Cadbury World in Birmingham. Numbered 93 in the fleet, and later re-registered KPR 698, this vehicle was the exception to the rule, carrying no HMS battleship name but simply being known as 'Chief' for obvious reasons! New vinyl graphics and metallic paints were becoming more common at this time, such artwork previously applied by hand. (Author's collection)

Another marque proving popular with the UK coach market at this time was the Beulas Stergo 'e' bodied Iveco Eurorider. Country Lion operated this example registered YNH 1W, which featured a metallic gold version of fleet livery. It was captured when new at Peterborough coach park on 13 October 2001, having dropped off a group attending a choir competition at the nearby cathedral. The registration mark was originally carried on a Ford Transit minibus and remains in use today on one of the company's double-deckers.

Minibuses and smaller coaches formed the majority of Country Lion's early fleet. A very rare combination was this twenty-eight-seat Reeve Burgess-bodied MAN 8.136, awaiting collection in August 1983 from dealers Moseley Continental who were purveyors of unusual vehicles. Period wheel trims feature and most of Country Lion's registration marks at this time featured only single or double digits. (Author's collection)

NT's pair of manual gearbox ECW-bodied Bristol LHs could once be seen operating infrequent cross-town route 6, which had been marketed as the 'Stage-coach service' long before Northamptonians had seen buses with stripes. Country Lion won the tender for the service in October 1992 and performing the duty on 1 September 1997 was Autobus Classique Nouvelle-bodied Mercedes-Benz L10 NCC, new to the company, laying over on Victoria Street. It can be noted the flags on the police and fire stations were at half-mast in respect of Princess Diana, whose funeral procession would visit the county on 6 September.

UC's final batch of Alexander RL-bodied Volvo Olympians, numbered 753–762, arrived in October 1998. These would also be the last step-entrance double-deckers to enter service and were licensed the same week as the low-floor Dennis Dart SLFs. 758 waits beside Little Houghton church on 3 September 1999 for pupils of Woolaston School. Later renumbered 16228 and utilised at Bedford depot on 'Biggleswade & District' school duties in a dedicated livery, further service would see it return to standard corporate colours with Strathtay and then Fife.

Yorks 50 (RBD 287Y, SYK 901, FNM 710Y), named 'HMS Manchester', was a Plaxton Supreme-bodied Ford acquired from Ralph's of Longford in November 1983. Laying over outside the company's Short Lane depot in Cogenhoe on 16 June 1997, while working the service bus Y4 duty, it would depart at midday for Northampton.

Just down the road from Cogenhoe were the premises of Wright's Trucks where, from 18 September 2005, MK Metro established a 'depot' within the yard for the six vehicles and ten drivers initially used on four contracted routes. Regular vehicles were allocated, which, at times, were interchanged with members of the main MK fleet. A treat for those on the principal University route 21 on 26 November 2005 was brand new long wheelbase thirty-seven-seat Optare Solo 33 (YJ55 YGW). One of a pair, it became 2450 under Arriva ownership.

Three Caetano Compass-bodied Dennis Dart SLFs were allocated to Northampton, numbered 62–64. All new to Limebourne in 1999 for TFL routes 42, 156 and 344, after a period in store they received a neat single-door conversion at Caetano's Waterlooville premises. Newly delivered and looking spruce on 16 November 2005, T425 LGP had been named 'Pendennis Castle' by its previous owner and later became 3535 with Arriva The Shires. The 'depot' can be viewed to the left of the turning area, which shows signs of the constant use by HGVs.

This unusual body style had been seen in Northampton before when in November 1998 Montague Euro, trading as A1 Taxis, began operating a small fleet of buses. Three vehicles with consecutive registrations were leased from Arriva, each with a different body and chassis combination. Piggy-in-the-middle was Dennis Dart SLF S402 JUA with Urban Star bodywork by UVG, the company name before Caetano's ownership. The operation didn't last long and the vehicles returned to their lessor, the example depicted joining five similar examples at North Kent Express in 1999 for use on a Millennium Dome Park & Ride contract. Chase of Walsall acquired the bus in 2001 where it was re-registered PSU 989 and eventually became Arriva Midlands 2382. (Author's collection)

In the 1990s the products offered by Caetano were favoured by Jeffs Coaches. The ever-reliable Volvo B10M was the chassis and ESU 635 (previously G908 WAY), which carried Caetano's Algarve bodywork, was one of thirty in the fleet. On 17 March 2002 it waits outside Grendon Hall for Stowe School students.

We join Yorks' Y4 service once more where the route's regular vehicle had been upgraded by this 16 June 1999 view at Salcey Rise, Piddington. Plaxton Paramount 3200-bodied Volvo B10M 54 (XVY 392, B711 PEC, LIB 3766, B196 MAO) was new to Stainton of Kendal, acquired in April 1995 and appropriately named 'HMS Cumberland'.

Competition with Stagecoach during the summer of 1993 took NT over the borough boundary to the Saxon village of Earls Barton. One of four new services introduced by NT, operating between 08.00 and 18.00 with a maximum fare of 40p, the 91 ran direct along the A4500 then made a loop around Dowthorpe Hill, part of the village not served by other bus routes. Departing Earls Barton Square half-hourly, Volvo B10M 112 (G112 ENV) picks up at Northampton Road by Elizabeth Way on 17 August 1993. NT would work through the village again from April 1996 on six contracts for schools in Wellingborough.

UC's service 47 from Irthlingborough to Northampton was regularly operated by the Northern Counties Palatine-bodied Volvo Olympians. Although the bus stop lay-bys at WFC were both extended, the facility would have greatly benefited from a small bus station. Picking up at the Emmanuel Church side, 679 carries a good load on 31 October 1997.

The X46 was launched on 2 April 2006 running direct to Earls Barton via the A45. The 'old road' (A4500) was served by half-hourly route 45, which ran to Irthlingborough. Simple branding was applied to several of this type as depicted on 16683. Further changes would see routes X4, X46 and 45 redesigned with the latter curtailed at Wellingborough and transferred to Kettering depot along with some of the buses. (Author's collection)

Eleven Transbus Tridents with ALX400 bodies were received in early 2006, with 18400 to 18406 being branded for the X46. On Sunday 4 May 2009 18403 (KX06 JYE) calls at Skinners Hill, Rushden, at 13.25 bound for Raunds. At the time of writing Northampton depot has become a Trident haven with examples originating from numerous Stagecoach UK depots.

Eight of the ARP-X batch of ECW-bodied Leyland Olympians were still in use at Northampton depot when 609 (ARP 609X) was caught at Woolaston School on 3 September 1999. The unreliable Transign destination blinds were replaced in the mid-1990s with almost every vehicle receiving a slightly different layout. The majority of this Bristol-built batch clocked up twenty years of service.

Immaculately presented 744 (LFJ 878W) loads at Kettering bus station, adjacent to the depot, on 29 June 1998. Routes 13/14/15 had several variants with the full route running to Bozeat, Grendon or Yardley Hastings. Thirteen Bristol VRs were then allocated to Kettering but an impending influx of Leyland Olympians would see 744 transfer to Bedford. Sold to Eston, Cleveland, in 2001, accident damage would see the bus withdrawn soon after.

Jointly operated with Viscount, the X65 provided an express between Northampton and Peterborough running via Kettering and Corby. 511 (F511 NJE) was part of a batch of twelve Northern Counties Palatine-bodied Leyland Olympians new to Cambus in 1988 and was departing Greyfriars bus station at 13.15 on 7 March 1997 for its home city, which would be reached two hours later. The Wayfarer 3 ticket machine hadn't long replaced aging 'Setright' equipment.

May 2000 saw the introduction of route X4, replacing the X65. Kettering depot operated a significant number of 'Coachlinks' services, the name still featuring on the side of 181, although the 'Stagecoach Express' brand should have been applied by the time of this 2 August 2000 view. The Plaxton Premiere Interurban-bodied Volvo B10M, one of thirteen delivered in November 1997, replaced older examples at Kettering, which were cascaded to other depots. Laying over at Peterborough railway station terminus this stop was handy for connections but, due to traffic congestion, departures would only be made from the nearby bus station.

Eleven Transbus ALX400-bodied Tridents were delivered to Kettering in 2004 to work on route X4, which, by then, operated half-hourly between MK and Corby, continuing hourly beyond there to Peterborough. 'Stagecoach Express' was replaced with 'Cross County' branding as depicted on 18109 (KX04 RVL), caught departing Queensgate bus station bay 15 at 17.10 on 5 April 2008. This glass-clad facility certainly had the greenhouse effect with the image of Westgate Church nicely reflected behind the bus. The Tridents were fitted with bus seats and although lacking certain refinements, reliably served the route for many years.

Stagecoach Group acquired Cambus Holdings (CHL Group) in December 1995 with operations in Cambridge, Peterborough and MK. A Monopolies & Mergers Commission ruling saw the MK operation and UC's Huntingdon depot sold to Julian Peddle, as we will see later. The need to upgrade the double-deck profile of their new acquisition saw Stagecoach lease fifty-two Northern Counties Palatine-bodied Volvo Olympians from 1996. These eighty-two seaters replaced a large fleet of Bristol VRs of differing heritage, with some also seeing use at UC depots when part of the east division. 541 represents the type at RAF Mildenhall Air Show on 26 May 2001 working P&R duties. Later converted to open top for City Sightseeing work and re-registered ACZ 7489, it became 16541 in the UK national numbering series.

Twelve of the P-EFL batch were retained by Stagecoach Group, equally split between Ely and Stratford-Upon-Avon, all others returning off-lease. Those remaining were converted to full or partial open top, with 15545 (WLT 908, P545 EFL) in Cambridge Tour City Sightseeing livery representing the latter at Ely depot. In May 2012 it assumed its original registration when it transferred to more rural surroundings with Stagecoach Orkney. (Raymond Bedford)

Stagecoach Express route X5 was launched on 25 September 1995 linking Cambridge and Oxford with an hourly headway. Six former Wallace Arnold coaches were initially used, allocated in pairs to Northampton, Bedford and Huntingdon depots. They were replaced in 1999 with Volvo B10Ms, previously on the Oxford Tube, the majority of which carried Jonckheere Deauville bodies. An exception was M105 XBW with Berkhof Excellence bodywork, others of this type being deployed on Virgin Trains contract VT99. Numbered 25 at Oxford, it became Northampton depot's 105 and was captured loading at MK Coachway on 27 December 1999 for its former home city.

Seven Optare Solos were delivered to Northampton depot in November 2004 for use on route '4U' in one last competitive move against NT. The period was brief and the additional services withdrawn a year later. Northampton retained the vehicles with six later receiving branding for Gold Star routes 88 and 89. These services, which should not be confused with the 'Stagecoach Gold' product, ran between Northampton and Towcester diverging at that town to either Oxford or MK. 47127 (KN54 XYV) was heading home along Midsummer Boulevard on 5 April 2008, revealing how this leafy, landscaped 'new city' looks rather bare during the winter months.

Services 86 and 87 were in effect two circular routes which served a great number of villages en route to their southern terminus of Towcester. MK Metro's rural rota crewed the routes from Wolverton depot with changeovers taking place at Marlow Road in Towcester. On 20 August 2005 109 had shuttled along Watling Street from MK, the driver awaiting the arrival of the 87, which departed Northampton at 14.53. The Plaxton Beaver 2-bodied Mercedes-Benz Vario was one of six new in September 1997 uniquely fitted with seatbelts for use on a school contract.

Once owned by Basfords Coaches, Jeffs ran from their Greens Norton High Street premises, which was home to NBD 309V, a Duple Dominant II-bodied Bedford YMTs new in 1980. Of the original seven, three were still active when this 29 April 2002 view was captured at Blisworth Hill lay-by off the A43. Having completed a school contract the vehicle was about to see use on a private hire taking a team from 'The Bull' in Towcester to Northampton Town FC's Sixfields Stadium to compete in a local pub league final.

Jeffs acquired several Leyland Olympians around the turn of the new millennium, mostly of City of Oxford origin. However, SCK 226X was one of a pair acquired from Blazefield Group's Burnley & Pendle and Lancashire United fleets. Beginning life as 2126 with Ribble, it was sold to Blazefield as part of a divestment of Lancashire operations in 2001. Rubbed down ready for repaint, the bus had been pressed into service on 31 May 2002 from Greens Norton depot.

In the 1980s Jeffs had an association with body builders Jonckheere, supplying their products from premises in Northampton under the name Roeselare. Carrying Jonckheere's Jubilee P599 bodywork was Scania K112 CRS, appropriately registered A112 SNH, acting as a demonstrator for the chassis manufacturer. The vehicle would soon be sold to Marshall's of Leighton Buzzard, a keen user of the type, and carry registrations SM 9562 and WJI 5277 during its life. (Author's collection)

Based at Helmdon was this unique twenty-nine-seat Indcar Maxim-bodied Iveco, which despite looking rather ungainly was a very comfortable vehicle. Having just dropped off Stowe School polo team in the nearby village of Inglesham it was caught resting at Lechlade in Gloucestershire on 3 March 2002. New in May 1999, the coach was later re-registered VVV 66S, a plate originally carried on an ex-NT Bristol VR.

A mix of dealer stock coaches were hired to Jeffs following a depot fire at Helmdon in which a number of vehicles were lost. Previously operating with Trafalgar was T713 UOS, a Volvo B10M with Jonckheere Mistral 50 bodywork. Some of the loaned vehicles were subsequently purchased. Note the rear of the Dennis Javelin parked alongside which, despite this view being taken on 26 April 2002, was still advising a depot phone number with pre 'phone day' dialling code.

By the mid-2000s the majority of UC's coach work was being performed by single- or double-deck buses. A coach joining in 2006 was 52644, a Volvo B10M with Jonckheere Mistral 50 bodywork, one of a pair new to Newcastle-based Busways in 1998 for Flightlink duties. Acquired from Mansfield depot, the vehicle mainly saw use on route X6 between Northampton and Oxford, which consisted of four return journeys. It soon moved to Bedford depot and on 8 March 2010 was departing Gloucester Green heading east on the X5. Interestingly the vehicle was never locally registered, carrying KSU 461 from new and later NDZ 3021 when with East Kent as a driver trainer. Northampton's other acquisition was Volvo B7R 53276.

By 2009 Oxford wasn't directly served by routes from Northampton depot, as service 8 terminated at Bicester. Two of Oxford's Alexander ALX300-bodied MANs, new in 1998, were transferred to Northampton and branded for this long and unusual cross-Northampton service. The number had previously applied to a route running from the bus station to Headlands and WFC, which was later joined to the Silverstone, Brackley and Bicester service. Did anyone ever travel end-to-end? 22920 was caught at Silverstone on 21 June 2009 whilst working special duties for the annual Formula One event.

The long-established link between Banbury and Brackley was route 500 in the numbering series, which had origins with Midland Red. Alexander ALX200-bodied Volvo B6BLE 31362 (P362 DSA) was branded for the service, and a map on the first nearside window detailed the simplistic nature of the route, which ran every thirty minutes. New to Stagecoach Glasgow as 362 in 1997, the bus was one of numerous examples in use by Midland Red South and was waiting to depart Banbury for another day's work on 26 November 2009. (Raymond Bedford)

Based in the rural Northamptonshire village of Eydon, Geoff Amos ran a long-established bus route between Banbury and Rugby, loosely following the path of the former Great Central Railway. Numbered GA01/GA02, Rural Bus Grant funding in 2000 saw the timetable improve and new low-floor vehicles were purchased. Further enhancements came in 2005 with a batch of MCV Evolution-bodied MANs joining the fleet, one of which, 53 (AM05 BUS), was caught at Bridge Street, Banbury, on 8 March 2010. The Egyptian-built bus would work the 12.10 departure, arriving at Rugby railway station at 14.13.

At Rugby railway station on 29 June 1987 we see unusual traction in the shape of Reeve Burgess-bodied Dennis Dorchester 51 (XAM 124A), new in December 1984. The seventy-one seater, which was later registered B368 KNH, wears the company's cream with purple relief livery and was one of four Dennis Dorchesters in use at the time. Rugby station has changed considerably following extensive refurbishment in 2006 and today the bus route is split into two, with both sections now run by Stagecoach following Amos' closure in 2011. (Kevin Lane/Author's collection)

Stagecoach Warwickshire's Rugby depot commenced operation of route 72 in September 2009. This hourly service was usually operated by two branded Dennis Dart SLFs formerly of Stagecoach East London. However, on 24 June 2010 ageing Alexander RL-bodied Leyland Olympian 14028 (F628 MSL) works the route at Clifton Road heading towards Daventry. New in September 1988 at Bedford's Biggleswade outstation, the bus passed to Rugby mid-2006 with five of the batch in use principally on school work. The Hannover dot-matrix blind was a later fitment and the bus would make Daventry its next home in 2011 with Hunter's Coaches.

Long-serving Northampton ECW-bodied Bristol VR 937 (SNV 937W) was one of ten remaining at the depot when this 8 January 1997 view was taken of it departing Greyfriars bus station. In hot pursuit is a Northampton Borough Council road sweeper, which had just completed its cycle of the bus station. New in August 1980, the bus has been working the two-hourly 'stopping service' 41 from Daventry.

The Daventry trunk routes were upgraded in April 2002, the X42 running direct and the 40 taking a more meandering path, both operating hourly. The 'X' would link the two towns' bus stations within thirty minutes. Lang Farm estate in Daventry was the route's ultimate destination where a member of the versatile ECW-bodied Leyland Olympian batch, 608 (ARP 608X), was heading soon after the route's introduction. The location is Speke Drive, Ashby Fleids. (Author's collection)

UC's final twenty-six Alexander AM-bodied Mercedes-Benz 709Ds received in May/June 1996 were more refined than their higher-numbered more elderly stablemates. Badged as 'Alexander Sprint', the bodywork was slightly wider, cab access was via the saloon and UC's examples had twenty-three dual-purpose type seats. Northampton was allocated three of the batch, with 303 laying over at Greyfriars on 16 September 1998. The Street Shuttle brand was still in use, with Daventry having its own network of town services, some routes making occasional trips to outlying villages.

September 2007 saw Northampton depot's Daventry area routes redesigned and relaunched as 'Daventry Dart', with the principal services making 'loops' of the town after initially serving the bus station. Nearby villages were covered by more infrequent routes, one of which, Plaxton Pointer-bodied Dennis Dart 32140 (L140 VRH), was operating on 30 April 2008. The thirty-four seater, new to East London in 1993 as DRL140, carries a good load from the bus station and offers a connection with National Rail services at its ultimate destination.

Eighteen slimline Optare Solos were delivered in 2006, principally for use on routes funded by Northamptonshire CC. Most wore the corporate livery with some carrying schemes for networks or individual route branding. 47418 (KX55 PGO) was based at Northampton and was the only such vehicle to wear the Daventry Dart brand. Having a day away on 16 September 2007 at Duxford Showbus, it had somehow erroneously ended up on display amongst the London vehicles.

Geoff Amos operated some interesting vehicles over the years as exemplified by this pair of double-deck coaches. Jonckheere Jubilee P99-bodied DAF SBR2300 (TOI 6161, A48 JLW) leads No. 64 (XAM 124A), a contemporary UK-built Plaxton Paramount 4000, which was also coupled to a DAF chassis. As inferred on the sides of both vehicles longer-distance work was their mainstay. (Colin Lloyd/Author's collection)

UC didn't receive any of Stagecoach Group's large batch of Alexander-PS bodied Volvo B10Ms from new. However, in 2006 a number were transferred from Manchester and Midland Red South as replacements for double-deck vehicles at Northampton and Bedford. From Rugby came 20202, which, on 8 July 2007, waits at Northampton railway station to operate special service F1 to Silverstone motor racing circuit. One of ten allocated to Northampton, they were well suited to the interurban routes upon which they worked.

Midland Red South's Rugby depot stopped serving Northampton from October 1999 when the services between the two towns were split at the county boundary. NT were awarded the contract for routes 207–210, which initially ran from the village of Crick to Northampton, keeping within the county. On 22 December 1999 Duple 300-bodied Volvo B10M G114 ENV awaits departure at 09.09 from the Posthouse Hotel at Crick.

On Saturdays two different route variations existed with none of the journeys connecting with the Midland Red South service, which then ran as far as West Haddon. Operating the last journey of the day, the 16.50 from Northampton, a touch of luxury featured on 12 August 2000 in the shape of Wright Axcess-Floline-bodied Scania L94 362 (V362 CNH). Setting down at the last stop in Long Buckby, the flag of which still carries Midland Red South details.

Having made a cautious trip to Northampton on route 88 from Rugby, DAF-repowered Leyland National 629 (PUK 629R) lays over on Victoria Street on the last day of 1996. The Mounts police and fire stations dominate the backdrop and this street is now classified as Northampton's coach station. Rugby's Leyland Nationals soldiered on until 2000. Today, Stagecoach once more operates between Northampton and Rugby.

A link to Leicester via Market Harborough was available on routes X60 and X61, which UC operated jointly with Midland Fox. Brightening up the Greyfriars gloom on 1 September 1997 was 33 (N433 XRC), an East Lancs European-bodied Scania L113CRL, the last of a batch of five new in 1996. City Rider was the trading name of Derby City Transport, then also part of the Cowie Group (later Arriva), who had loaned the vehicle to Midland Fox. UC's journeys at the time were joined to the former X38 route to Oxford and ran as through services.

By 1999 Midland Fox only ran between Leicester and Market Harborough, although such short workings had existed previously, some numbered X62 and running via Foxton. All Fox journeys would appear in UC's publicity material until 2000. Their varied fleet ensured some unusual types would feature such as Wigston-based Leyland National 2 EON 829V, numbered 3829, captured among the period concrete styling of Leicester city centre. New to Midland Red as 829, it moved within the British Bus Group to Colchester in January 1994. (Author's collection)

Former Midland Red South Alexander PS-bodied Volvo B10M 20217 (P217 HBD) was branded for the hourly X7 while based at Northampton. Here we see it approximately halfway home at Market Harborough on 10 June 2008. The route was once part of the Coachlinks network and became 'Stagecoach Express' when renumbered to X7, a Best Impressions-designed timetable book accompanying the 2002 relaunch. The Volvos were well suited to the X7 and were regular performers on the route for several years.

Kettering depot drivers also reached Market Harborough on the infrequent route 17. On 10 June 2008 Northern Counties-bodied Leyland Olympian 14064 loads at Market Hall for the 10.03 departure, which would meander through some picturesque Northamptonshire villages on its way home. New in 1992 at Northampton depot, the bus looked spruce, although its original headlights had by now been replaced. An analogue tachograph unit was fitted to the bus, which saw occasional use on the long X4 service. At this time Northampton depot operated an infrequent route also numbered 17, which served Billing Aquadrome.

At the same location on the same day we meet the operations of French-owned Veolia Group, which rapidly acquired a number of smaller firms across the UK during the mid-2000s including the local bus operations of Paul James Coaches. Painted in the Group's corporate colours, a Plaxton Beaver 2-bodied Mercedes-Benz Vario works a town service. By 2013 most of Veolia's bus and coach operations in the UK had been sold.

From April 1996 much variety featured in NT's fleet to fulfil newly won contracts. This included 20 (WSV 144, A13 SMT, E353 KSF), one of two smart Duple 340-bodied Leyland Tigers from Midland Bluebird. New to Eastern Scottish as YL353, the fifty-three seater wore a GRT-inspired coach livery and the pair's modern styling made them suitable for private hire duties. With that in mind this 1997 publicity shot was taken at the recently opened Brixworth Country Park. The vehicle also carried the identity NTL 655. (St Giles Photography/Author's collection)

Alexander RL-bodied Volvo Olympian 699 (R699 DNH) entered service from Northampton depot in November 1997. Having run 'dead' from Greyfriars on 26 August 1999 to the specific location of No. 42 Brixworth Road, Creaton, as shown in the timetable, it would depart at 08.54 for Northampton. Every journey on route 62 was different and a whole host of codes was detailed at the bottom of the timetable. The bus was the first to receive the 'swoops' livery in January 2001 and uniquely 'Stagecoach serving Northampton' lettering was applied instead of 'Northants'. It worked Northampton's last Volvo Olympian day on 20 August 2016 after which it was sold locally to Marshalls of Leighton Buzzard.

NT began operation on route 60 to Guilsborough in March 1987 initially using Leyland National number 25. Duple 300-bodied Volvo B10M 111 would soon upgrade the allocation, but with extra capacity required for the carriage of school children East Lancs-bodied Bristol VRs would eventually be used. In this 1994 view at Chapel Brampton 74 (ABD 74X), new in January 1982, is town-bound. By this time only three of the original batch of six remained. (David Pike)

On 24 April 2003 during the Easter school holiday, the route was being operated by one of First Northampton's Volvo B6s. Northern Counties Paladin-bodied 434 (L6 GML) was new in March 1994 to Gatwick Motors for airport car park shuttle work. Its extra luggage racks are still fitted despite having also worked with First Capital Citybus. Leaving Northampton at 08.14, it was seen running along a narrow road linking Guilsborough to the main West Haddon Road, upon which it would continue to Cold Ashby and Welford. This was the penultimate day of NT operation, with Centrebus about to take over the contract.

Several stately homes are to be found between Northampton and Market Harborough, one such example being Cottesbrooke Hall and Gardens. On 23 September 2000 several NT vehicles were hired by Phoenix Computers to convey guests to an event being held on-site. The driver of Plaxton Paramount 3500-bodied Volvo B10M 11 (SSU 837, G427 PWW, 8995 WY, G73 RGG) is being directed away from soft ground where a fellow coach had become stuck! Its cherished registration plate, which originated with Midland Bluebird, is still used by Tamworth Bus & Coach.

Northamptonshire's seasonal 'Saunterbus' was a network of County Council-funded services operating between April and September, which linked attractions and places of interest around the county that were not always accessible by bus. Both NT and UC had operated the contract with most of the journeys running on Sundays. Caught operating the 'Rutland Saunter' at Oakham on 3 June 2001 was UC's Alexander RL-bodied Volvo Olympian 695, which had meandered its way from Northampton to serve the town and nearby Rutland Water.

From the original batch of nine Alexander AM-bodied Mercedes-Benz 709Ds, which featured the earlier body styling, 354 (K354 ANV) was captured at George Street in Corby wearing an overall advert for a local VW dealership. Minibuses in Corby at the time were painted black and gold and branded 'Magic Minis', taking over the main town services previously operated by Routemasters. Both these very different products sought to compete with the significant number of London-style Hackney Carriages plying for hire in the town, some of which are in evidence in the backgound. (Author's collection)

The 'Corby Star' brand was launched in June 2003 using eleven Optare Solos, which, in April 2004, were joined by five East Lancs Omnidekka-bodied Scania N94UDs. They were UC's first low-floor double-deckers, arriving seven years after the 'S' registered Volvo Olympians were delivered. Northamptonshire County Council sponsored the network and influenced vehicle specification, hence a type unfamiliar to Stagecoach. However, they replaced several former East London Leyland Titans, which were perhaps equally as unusual. Last of the batch, 15405 (KX04 RDV), carried branding for cross-town route 3, although the buses were utilised on all town and some rural services. The vehicle was seen amongst a mass of cars and buses at Hinton Airfield P&R site on 21 June 2009, working a duty for the Silverstone F1 event. Members of the batch were still serving north Northamptonshire in 2022.

Arguably UC's first low-floor double-deck buses could be considered a batch of seven Dennis Tridents with stylish Plaxton President bodywork delivered in December 2000. The Northampton-registered vehicles, equally unusual for the Stagecoach Group, were received when UC, Cambus and Viscount jointly operated as Stagecoach East. They were the first vehicles in the area delivered in the new corporate livery and 707 (X707 JVV) had become 17697 by the time of this 9 June 2008 view, reversing off the stand at Drummer Street bus station. The university cities of Oxford and Cambridge both had modern bus stations with small aprons, making manoeuvrability tricky. The bus was one of four later transferred to Stagecoach Midlands and used at Corby and Kettering.

Earlier we saw the bold and bright overall advert used by Airflow, their choice of colour scheme having become more sedate by the time of this 25 July 1999 view. Three overall schemes were carried for Airflow on the Northern Counties Palatine-bodied vehicles based at Northampton. 673 was viewed at Newland Street in Kettering about to work the unusual Sunday-only 17.27 departure to Northampton and Beacon Bingo on route X64. Surprisingly, there was no direct return journey.

ECW-bodied Bristol VR 862, new in March 1977, led a nomadic life operating from all UC depots before joining the 'low mileage' fleet in summer 1993. Still clocking up mileage when working from Kettering, on 7 August 1997 it was seen resting between journeys on the main 'stopping' service from Northampton. Although on an hourly frequency, the route had numerous variations making for a fussy-looking timetable. After a final stint with Bedford depot the bus was withdrawn on 5 November 1998.

In August 1989 UC received eleven Alexander RL-bodied Leyland Olympians, of which five featured coach seats and all were registered in the G-EVV series. 643 had been used by Northampton depot from new and transferred to Kettering in December 1997. Frequently returning to its former home, on 17 February 2001 it loads at the bus stop by the White Elephant pub on Kettering Road. It wasn't clear which route the red Vauxhall Nova was operating! Later renumbered 14043, the bus remained at Kettering until December 2010 when it was sold to Cooper's of Grimsby.

In 2005 the principal Northampton to Kettering route was reorganised and co-ordinated with new route 38, a route number previously associated with the service to Towcester. After serving Moulton the 38 ran to Wellingborough and the 39 to Kettering, each offering an hourly headway. Any type of vehicle could work the routes, with 16688 on the 38 arriving back at Greyfriars in early 2007. Note the sign on the bus station wall which pedestrians would have to cross the roadway to read! (Nigel Wheeler)

Uno (formerly University Bus) of Hatfield began operating in Northampton from September 2012 on routes centred on the university which had previously been operated by Soul's Coaches. Commercial routes were also established and additional contracts gained including rural route 37 to and from Hannington. On 17 June 2015 DP122 (SN51 TAU) was running dead to that village to take up the 10.30 journey to Northampton and pauses briefly at Walgrave war memorial, a stop not served by any service at the time. The Plaxton Pointer 2-bodied Dennis Dart SLF was one of several acquired from London United and was previously Fulwell garage's DPS579.

With the acquisition of CHL Group came coach division Premier Travel, who operated several National Express contracts. Eight Plaxton Expressliner 2-bodied Volvo B10Ms were received in 1995 just prior to the Stagecoach takeover. Leader of the batch was London-branded 445, named 'Spirit of Kings Lynn', seen loading at Kettering bus station on 7 August 1997 for the 12.55 departure on route 314. Three return journeys ran from Cambridge to Birmingham on this cross-country route, which utilised the newly opened A14. Cambridge Coach Services competed with routes 70 and 71, which also served Kettering on the way to Birmingham or Worcester. The coach would later become 52295 and transfer to West Scotland. Route number 314 was later assigned to the Cambridge to Liverpool service, which ran through Bedford and Northampton.

UC's involvement with National Express work ended in September 1998 when the four routes operated were transferred to fellow Group company Midland Red South's Rugby depot. Five Plaxton Premiere 350-bodied Volvo B10Ms had been used, three transferring to East Midlands and the other two to Rugby. The Rugby pair included 95 (J446 HDS), which is receiving external bodywork attention at Kettering on 29 June 1998.

Travelling south from Northampton we soon arrive at the new city of Milton Keynes where the MK Citybus brand name, which originated with NBC, had become more prominent on the run-up to privatisation. By the end of 1987 ninety-two Mercedes-Benz minibuses had replaced all but a handful of conventional vehicles, which had been retained for certain peak hour journeys and contracts. Three Bristol VRT3s were sold to Brighton & Hove in the cull but, surprisingly, mark 2 VR GNJ 575N was acquired from B&H in July 1988. Numbered 3575, it was seen at MK Central railway station in November 1990 wearing the drab white and cream livery initially used by the company. The more pleasing green and cream scheme was later applied, with the bus eventually scrapped in 1996. (Bob Jackson collection)

Representing one of the ninety-two Mercedes-Benz 608Ds is 0050 (D150 VRP) laying over at Central bus station in December 1988. Its Alexander AM bodywork looking somewhat battle-scarred, it was one of six to have nineteen coach seats fitted and wear the coach livery variant. Its route number had originated with UC for the Stony Stratford to Bletchley service, and such numbers were still carried on peak hour workings, the main 'Street Shuttle' network simply being numbered 1 to 8. Several of the batch would leave the city's roundabouts behind for new homes in North Wales – Alpine Coaches in this case. (Author's collection)

Under Julian Peddle's ownership steady and continual investment was made and from 1997 the Mercedes-Benz Vario would replace older inherited stock. Twenty-six of the type would eventually be used, all featuring Plaxton's Beaver 2 bodywork. 128 (V128 UNH), the last new example, was registered on 20 August 1999 and the only such vehicle to carry a V-plate. These versatile Varios would often be seen on rural routes such as Northamptonshire CC supported 86 and 87, upon which a full circuit took almost two hours. Viewed on 20 August 2005 at Bridge Street in the tourist hotspot of Stoke Bruerne, the dot matrix blind was a later addition. The bus would become 2306 with Arriva The Shires.

Of the twenty-six Mercedes-Benz Varios operated eight were acquired second hand, five of which came from Trent. The last to be acquired was R828 WBC, new to Trent's Kinch Bus division, replacing a similar vehicle at MK which had sustained accident damage. Travelling on trade plates to its new home on 30 August 2005, it approaches Grafton Regis. Receiving the number 124, it would soon be repainted into the company's yellow and blue livery, which it would retain during Arriva ownership.

Under CHL Group ownership five Leyland National 2s were transferred from Cambridge, originating with Eastern Counties in 1980. Their image featured on timetable and publicity material and they saw regular use on one time Johnson's Coaches route 33 between MK and Northampton. At the start of 1996 only three Leyland National 2s and seven Bristol VRs remained in service. All would be withdrawn at the beginning of the new MK Metro era with 2622, pictured alongside a fellow vehicle, passing to Barnsley & District. Interestingly, Bletchley depot had been the recipient of UC's first batch of Leyland National 2s in 1980. (Author's collection)

An early purchase by MK's new owners, and a forerunner for many more unusual astute acquisitions was 458 (H858 NOC), a Carlyle Dartline-bodied Dennis Dart new in 1991 to D&J of Silvertown, where it had been used on London City Airport duties. Still to dual-door configuration when pictured on 7 July 1997, about to enter Northampton's Drapery, its thirty-two coach seats would later be replaced, the bus converted to single door and a destination blind retrofitted.

A smart livery variation and simple branding was launched in 2004 for quality route 5. On Monday to Saturday a city-bound journey carrying that number originated at Hartwell, with two return journeys on Sunday numbered 33 reaching Hanslope. UC operated the full service on route 33 at the time and on 29 May 2005 a rather unusual vehicle is ready for the 14.00 departure from Hanslope Square. 61 (YG52 CMU) had been recently acquired from Cumbrae Coaches of Millport, on the Isle of Cumbrae. Square headlights and auxiliary heaters distinguished this vehicle from a pair of similar Wright Cadet 2-bodied VDL SB120s new to MK Metro, although 61 was badged as a DAF. Becoming 3731 with Arriva The Shires, it carried coats of many colours at MK and later transferred to Arriva Midlands' training fleet as 9549.

UC's main routes linking Northampton to MK were numbered 34 to 38, each with variants on most journeys on different days of the week. ECW-bodied Bristol VR 735 (LFJ 864W) was new as Devon General 1217 and is nearing journeys end heading along Drapery on 6 August 1997. The 37 served villages off the A5 and A508, six return journeys operating during off-peak hours six days a week, with no provision on Sundays. The bus would migrate with others to Bedford depot and was scrapped in June 2000.

Passing through the village of Yardley Gobion on 23 September 1999 Alexander Sprint-bodied Mercedes Benz 709D 303 (N303 XRP) was working a journey on route 37, scheduled as part of an MK outstation duty. Vehicles from Northampton and Bedford were outstationed at MK Metro's Winterhill depot and used by MK-based drivers on a wide variety of routes.

MK Metro's 1 group of routes had varying ultimate destinations, the 1B covered one-time Yorks Y1 service, which had been numbered 36/A by UC. On 20 August 2005 Optare Solo 2, one of the company's original four delivered in January 1999, would depart MK Central railway station stop 33 at 08.36 for Northampton. The usual pattern was to then operate a short working to Piddington, Hackleton or Wootton Fields from Greyfriars bay 3, before the journey back to MK. The bus would later become 2432 with Arriva The Shires.

The 1B served the historic North Buckinghamshire town of Olney where we meet the operations of Souls Coaches, long associated with the town. September 2010 saw the company take over University of Northampton contracts from Arriva/MK Metro when that company closed their Billing outstation. General coach work was still the main operation, however, as represented by smartly presented Plaxton Paramount 3500-bodied Volvo B10M FAZ 4494, formerly F418 DUG, acquired in 1995 from The Londoners, Nunhead.

Wearing an overall advert for Northamptonshire Chamber of Commerce, UC's ECW-bodied Leyland Olympian 610 (ARP 610X) was caught standing in the main parking area of MK Metro's Winterhill depot on 11 September 1999. The site was soon to close and a Homebase store now occupies the area. With original Transign blinds still fitted, 610, later numbered 14010, along with eight others of the batch, would 'fly the standard of success' at Northampton depot until 2004. Luton & District's examples, which could also be seen in the area when operating from Aylesbury depot, were withdrawn in 2000/1. 610 would later be fitted with a Bristol VR-style front and was in use with Cooper's of Sheffield as late as 2009.

Transit Holdings were famed for their love of vehicles with dual-door layout, with L711 JUD new as 3002 in Oxford. After acquisition by the Stagecoach Group it also saw use at Barking and Basingstoke depots. MK Metro acquired three of this batch in 2003 with 416, as depicted, becoming a driver training vehicle; vinyls to such effect were added later. Perhaps a little less exotic than its predecessors, which included a Leyland PD3, Bristol LH and Leyland National, it takes a break from tuition at Bleak Hall depot on 9 July 2005. The instructor's crew seat can be seen through the entrance doors. This was removable and with the addition of a ticket machine the bus could be used on service work if required.

Traditionally, training vehicles were of a more time-expired nature and a challenge to drive. ECW-bodied Bristol LH SVL 834R was new to Lincolnshire Road Car in April 1977 numbered 1049, and joined Stagecoach through acquisition of Busways. In April 1998 it and two others joined UC and was allocated to Corby depot. Testing was conducted in-house with test routes around Northampton, including Greyfriars bus station 'express bays', which were used for the reverse/park manoeuvre in full view of waiting passengers! In this 27 May 1999 view the trainee is perhaps being shown the finer points of Greyfriars staff canteen!

Between 1993 and 2003 Bedford depot ran the majority of UC's Alexander Dash-bodied Volvo B6s. As we saw earlier, Northampton depot ran some examples including leader of the pack 401 (L401 JBD) seen on Billing Brook Road approaching WFC on 31 October 1997. Type familiarisation for drivers still in the training school was carried out as and when suitable vehicles were available. With all training buses at this time fitted with manual gearboxes this would have been an easier day for the trainee driver.

Vehicles retained for driver training duties would often remain on the books long after most of their contemporaries had been withdrawn, NT's 154 being such an example. New in June 1947, this Northern Coachbuilders-bodied Daimler CVG6 was the training bus for many years and numerous 'Corporation' drivers were put through their paces in this classic machine. Later utilised as a publicity vehicle, it was present at the opening ceremony of Greyfriars bus station in 1976. When this view was captured at St James depot in July 1993 it was soon to pass into preservation prior to the company's privatisation and is now in the safe hands of Northampton Transport Heritage. (Nigel Wheeler)

In 2007 UC were awarded school contracts on behalf of parent-run bus associations in the towns of Biggleswade and Shefford and two livery variations on the national scheme were applied to six Alexander RL-bodied Volvo Olympians. New to Northampton depot as 753 in November 1998 S753 DRP, now numbered 16223, was one of a trio in the Shefford & District scheme. These relatively youthful vehicles would also undertake service work and here a pupil-free day is being enjoyed at Showbus, Duxford, on 16 September 2007. All would return to standard fleet livery when the contracts were lost.

Prior to fifteen of UC's coaches becoming dedicated for school work a 'demonstration' vehicle was borrowed from Cwmbran depot. Wearing this smart red and white colour scheme, Plaxton Premiere Interurban-bodied Volvo B10M 52402 had been converted to seat seventy passengers in a 3+2 layout with seatbelts also fitted. Heading to Northampton on 18 February 2007, the coach was shown to local interested parties the following day, who clearly liked the concept.

The fledgling Stagecoach company saw great potential in the Routemaster and following privatisation several companies within the group operated the type. UC received seventeen and used them at Bedford and Corby depots between 1988 and 1993. None wore 'stripes' in service with the majority painted in UC's green livery and appropriately branded 'Routemaster'. Following withdrawal from service UC retained six, which were stored at Northampton, two of which (703 and 708) became special event vehicles. New as LT's RM682 (WLT 682), 703 was re-registered HVS 937 whilst at Bedford. Now wearing stripes on 14 July 1997, it was seen at Midland Red South's Banbury depot whilst on an enthusiasts' outing. Regrettably all six RMs were sent to PVS Barnsley for scrap on 18/19 March 1999.

As the Routemaster and Bristol VR chapters ended at Northampton the Bristol FLF made a comeback! A pair of ECW-bodied Bristol FLFs of Eastern Counties origin arrived with the merger of UC, Cambus and Viscount. Open-top JAH 552D was kept at Oundle depot with closed-top JAH 553D, making Northampton its new home. An 'FLF weekend' was held on 7 and 8 September 2002 on service 43 to Harpole and the main cross-town routes 1 and 51. Working the latter at Limehurst Square, Duston detailed the attractive Golden Jubilee livery which featured on both buses and was later applied to vehicles at Stagecoach Lincolnshire. Carrying various fleet numbers the pair were latterly 19952 based at Ely and 19953 at Kettering.

A decade later we celebrated the Queen's Diamond Jubilee and London hosted the Olympics. Stagecoach Group were awarded the operation to transport athletes and media around the metropolis, and significant logistical challenges for both vehicles and staff would be experienced. For consistency only vehicles with ADL chassis would be utilised with double-deckers for the Olympics and single-deckers for the Paralympics. In preparation at Upton Park garage on 12 August 2012 members of Northampton's Enviro 300 batch, numbered 27681–6, are seen in company with those from several other UK depots. Bombardier were converting the main section of the bus to carry four wheelchairs with each vehicle's seats placed on pallets and stored. This was the former LT garage's swansong having been mothballed leading up to the event and demolished soon after.

A significant number of short-term loans and transfers took place during the summer of 2012, not only from operational fleets but also from the large number of stored vehicles, which would otherwise have been withdrawn but were retained to cover the additional Olympic vehicle requirements. With Winchester's ADL Enviro-300s sent to London at short-notice, Northampton loaned Stagecoach South similar-looking 28621–27 with Scania K230UB chassis. Used from 5 August on P&R work, they also saw service at Portsmouth during September, mainly working route 23. Four were returning to Northampton on a damp 23 September 2012 and are seen taking a break at Cherwell Valley Services.

On loan to Stagecoach South's Chichester depot from Northampton's special event fleet was ECW-bodied Bristol FLF JAH 553D, seen in the grounds of Goodwood Estate on 17 September 2011 wearing standard corporate colours with matching interior trim. Working between Chichester railway station and the period-themed Goodwood Revival site, other Stagecoach heritage fleet buses were also in use on the popular revenue-earning service alongside a few privately preserved examples.

A significant date in Northamptonshire's calendar is the annual Formula 1 event held at Silverstone Racing Circuit. Stagecoach has been principal transport provider for many years with several P&R sites used and a special bus service in operation throughout the weekend. In 2007 additional duties included transporting marshals and trackside officials around the circuit itself. Alexander-RL-bodied Leyland Olympian 14047 (G647 EVV) waits on the grid prior to the qualifying race (for the cars!) on 6 July 2007. New as 647 in October 1989, fitted with coach seats, it was one of a pair used from Northampton on Coachlinks duties and private hire.

The same six vehicles had to be used on trackside duties with their chassis being thoroughly scrubbed prior to use as nothing could spill onto the tarmac! On 6 July 2007 Northern Counties-bodied 16675 (L675 HNV) could have remained on the circuit and kept pace with Lewis Hamilton and others as these Volvo Olympians gave a very lively performance! Note the event sponsor's transitioning titles displayed on boards along the pit straight.

After the qualifying race on 7 July 2007 16692 (P692 JBD) waits for the security gate to be opened to allow it to return home. Serving at Northampton depot until 2013, during its career it had been stolen from Greyfriars by 'joyriders', sustaining extensive damage, and later de-roofed under a railway bridge at Kibworth whilst in service. Due to an administrative error by DVLA three of the P-JBD batch were incorrectly registered when delivered, with the vehicle pictured originally carrying identity P691 JBD.

The 2007 race was a sell-out, 'Hamilton mania' resulting in large numbers of spectators attending the event. Route F1 was registered for operation over the weekend running from Northampton railway station to Silverstone village, buses returning via local back roads to start subsequent journeys. Northampton depot was one of the last in the Stagecoach Group to have vehicles running in the 'old' striped livery as exemplified by 16695 (R695 DNH) loading in the railway station car park.

For the main 2002 F1 event on Sunday 7 July Stagecoach sub-contracted thirty vehicles to First Northampton. These were for the Hinton Airfield P&R and even included Leyland Atlanteans and Gasbuses. With very limited Sunday work scheduled from St James depot a large pool of drivers was available at short notice. Volvo Citybus 290 waits at the 'Garage out' bus stop for departure of the convoy and still wears the red and cream livery variation and local name. One of the first to have this style applied to it would be one of the last to carry it. None of the extra buses were required on the day and most were back home before the race even started!

The most significant operation was P&R on the main race day, commencing in the early hours of the morning from three sites. A route from MK was later developed and Megabus began offering services from numerous destinations to the event, bookings made via the internet. Plaxton Expressliner 2-bodied Volvo B10M 52453 (R553 JDF) was new to the Cheltenham & Gloucester division in September 1997 for National Express contracts. Later seeing service from Bedford on the X5, it returned to C&G for use on Megabus work and later as a driver trainer. Here it is resting at Silverstone on 19 June 2009, the year the routes were launched.

Northampton's annual Balloon Festival was a popular event usually held a week after a similar show in Bristol. P&R sites at the University, Sixfields and Delapre Abbey were used and jointly operated by NT and UC. Leicester Citybus was in the process of receiving several Alexander RL-bodied Volvo Olympians from Glasgow in mid-2000, with some loaned short term to Northampton. P188 TGD had been numbered VO88 in Scotland and was used in as-acquired condition on route C at Park Campus on 18 August 2000. Becoming 34288 in First's national scheme, it would also see service in Essex, Worcester and lastly Stoke-on-Trent, eventually being scrapped in April 2014.

Later combined with the annual Town Show, numbers attending the event in 2007 were considerably less than in its heyday, with UC only offering a very limited P&R service. New in September 1988 at Bedford depot as 629, Leyland Olympian 14029, then allocated to Northampton, awaits the first departure from Walter Tull Way roundabout on 18 August 2007. This bus stop location was only suitable when the area was first built in 1993 with a lesser volume of passing traffic. Newly opened car parks along Edgar Mobbs Way link road were served that weekend.

Greater vehicle availability on Sunday 19 August 2007 saw more modern vehicles in use on both routes. Badging of Dennis products offered with Alexander's single- and double-deck ALX range changed over the period, although all kept the same appearance. 18409 (KX06 JYA) was an ADL ALX400-bodied ADL Trident hoping for some custom at the Racecourse Balloon Festival site.

Route 43 served the village of Harpole located just outside the borough boundary to the west of the town, and had previously been operated by UC. On 11 September 2005 the new contractor, MK Metro, ran a special one-off Sunday-only service 43A. Five return journeys between Greyfriars (bay 12) and the village were performed by unusual Optare Spectra-bodied DAF DB250 K302 FYG. Double-deckers were few and far between at MK Metro and Wolverton-based 202 was awaiting the 14.40 departure from Harpole Church, the village holding its annual Scarecrow Festival that weekend. New as London Buses SP2, with dual-doors, it was acquired in single-door configuration from Bennett's of Gloucester in 2001. Later becoming 6038 with Arriva The Shires, it would return to a red-based livery once more with Jan's of Soham.

A comparison can be made between LT's Routemaster styling and that of its 'provincial' equivalent with this open-top duo at All Saints Church, Harpole High Street. By the time of this 9 September 2007 view only MK Metro served Harpole, with the Stagecoach ECW-bodied Bristol FLF simply performing a circuit of the village, which was again decorated with scarecrows that weekend.

In 1991 seven Leyland Olympians were transferred from Northern Scottish, with a further six from Fife and four from Bluebird arriving in 1994, most allocated to Bedford. 708 was a short-wheelbase Leyland Olympian originating with Fife, carrying a different style of Alexander bodywork to the majority of UC's fleet. On 26 May 2001 the Bedford-based bus was one of many operating P&R duties from RAF Lakenheath to RAF Mildenhall for the annual air show. It retained its Fife fleet number with UC in the series previously used by Routemasters and later carried national number 14708. It was sold to Whippet Coaches in 2008.

Also providing transport for spectators to the air show at RAF Mildenhall, this time from Newmarket Racecourse, was Northampton's 759 (S759 DRP), later numbered 16229. It was the only vehicle used on the day of the event, 26 May 2001, to wear the new livery and only one of two UC double-deckers at the time to carry it. During its service from Bedford depot the bus received the special Biggleswade & District Bus Association themed school bus livery and later saw service with Rennies of Dunfermline.

Northampton town and the attractions on offer in the county have featured in the tour programmes of local and national coach companies large and small. Shire Coaches of St Albans' Berkhof Excellence-bodied Dennis Javelin P479 FAN awaits the return of its party at Mercers Row on Wednesday 6 August 1997. This was a market day, a popular day to visit, and a daily *Chronicle & Echo* newspaper could still be purchased from one of several street vendors, one of which was positioned by the escalators at Greyfriars.

Usually confined to adjacent Victoria Street or a nearby truck stop due to departure charges being applied, Wallace Arnold's 831 (K831 HUM) has chosen to layover at Greyfriars on 20 August 1993. The well-known firm had recently switched its bodywork supplier from Plaxton to some more exotic marques, which included Jonckheere's Deauville 45 as depicted. The Volvo B10M chassis was still favoured and one of this batch of twenty would later work for local operator Hunsbury Travel.

One operator booked to use Greyfriars 'express bays' was Polish-based Sindbad, who established a number of routes across the UK to Polish towns and cities. Their advantage over National Express-owned Eurolines was a greater list of local pick-up points. The crews of these smart Volvo and Mercedes coaches were using the facilities at Watford Gap services on 17 March 2009.

By 2006 Alexander RL-bodied Volvo Olympian 16221 was based at Bedford and received this attractive livery to mark eighty-five years since the formation of UC. Traditional liveries applied to modern vehicles add interest to any fleet and evoke memories perhaps as much as annual trips to Duxford for the Showbus rally, where the bus was on display on 24 September 2006.

Yorks' Northern Counties-bodied Maudslay FJ 6154 was new to Exeter Corporation in March 1929 and acquired in October 1965 from Arden of Haldon. Restored to excellent condition, it carried Yorks' traditional livery and fleet names when exhibited at the Northampton Town Show, Abington Park, on 20 July 1997. It had been brought to the event on a low-loader and spent most of its time stored undercover at the Cogenhoe premises. In November 2011 it passed for continued preservation with the West Country Historic Omnibus and Transport Trust.

As traditional liveries were being painted over in the late 1980s and 1990s who would have thought at the time we would one day see preserved vehicles wearing Stagecoach stripes. The scheme can be seen applied to many preserved examples including this Northamptonshire-associated pair at Buses Festival, Gaydon, on 18 August 2019. Alexander PS-bodied Volvo B10M 20202 was new to Midland Red South at Rugby numbered 202 in May 1995, joining Northampton depot in February 2007. UC Leyland Olympian 654, later 14054, was new in October 1990 and worked at Kettering and Bedford depots. Morton's Coaches of Tadley acquired it in 2011, the bus eventually becoming part of their heritage fleet when the stripes were applied.